# Heart Line

A collection of poems

Tasangkala Imchen

BookLeaf Publishing

India | USA | UK

Presentation by *BookLeaf Publishing*

Web: www.bookleafpub.com

E-mail: info@bookleafpub.com

ISBN:9789360943240

First edition 2024

*Dedicated to my dear mum who has left a legacy of prayer, faith and hard work. Dedicated to her because she taught me how to be a better person, daughter to my dad, and a caregiver to people in need.*

# ACKNOWLEDGEMENT

First and foremost, I would like to thank BookLeaf Publishing for such a platform that has made me an author by just stumbling upon social media.

I have always wanted to write poems and wished to turn them into a book, but I was too embarrassed to do so. And look what I have finally achieved !!!

Secondly, I am thankful to have experienced a few things in life that were worth putting into words and now in a book.

Thirdly, I thank my God for allowing me to be an inspiration to many. All the experiences in life that are now turning into a collection of poems, and ultimately, into a book, is an amazing experience altogether.

# PREFACE

This book called HEART LINE is a collection of poems that have been written in a span of 13 years about life's lessons, and people close to me, life as it is, and thoughts I can't share verbally with others.

Most of the poems are very personal but I felt it was worth being read by others and be blessed, inspired and realized.

Some of the poems would also talk about my relationship with God and nature.

Overall, these poems are my heart lines, which simply means speaking my heart out.

# Nature's Reflection

Through the four square window,
Behold the bushes,
Assorted in shapes and sizes,
With hues of green, brown, yellow, and red.

Do you perceive unity?
Do you discern the beauty in variety?
Are they not singular?
Yet, content and growing side by side.
Can you not see?

Could this be you?
Embrace individuality,
Embrace uniqueness,
Yet, stand together.

Ultimately, God's love for us knows no bounds!

# It is forever DECEMBER

Three Decembers have passed,
Yet I await another December,
For something enchanting.

In the first December,
You confessed your fondness,
Revealing a sentiment harbored for a decade.
I chuckled, questioning the timing,
After all these years.
Your response echoed,
"I lacked the courage to reveal it before!"

Then arrived the second December,
Your unexpected visit,
Followed by plans for a road trip.

The rest unfolded as history...

In the third December,
An unease settled between us,
Not because we were new acquaintances,
But because we were drifting apart.

I set you free!

Yet, you returned!

Two days elapsed,
And one evening, you appeared again,
With yet another surprise,
Declaring, "You're my confidant,
And I contemplate marriage with you!"
Do you recall?

I wait, still waiting,
For the fourth December,
Perhaps you'll propose,
"Let's tie the knot!"

I've marked each passing weekend,
Tallying up to ten,
...now, I've lost track of the count.

My dreams blur into uncertainty,
Yet, last night,
once more,
You visited my slumber,
Whispering something,
About us being debt-free upon marriage!

I'll inquire, come December,
When you seek my hand,
I'll question the validity of my vision.
Come December,
And my answer will be YES!
But wait…time will tell!

# December never came

December never arrived,
Marked the passing days,
Then weeks,
Christmas ensued,
And so did the New Year!

Yet now,
It holds no significance,
Four years squandered,
Tears shed in vain,
Prayers uttered to no avail,
Hope dwindled into despair,
Dreams dashed against reality,
Naive anticipation!

Endless waiting,
Clutching to the belief of redemption,
Yearning to prove doubters mistaken!

However...

Perhaps,
They were, absolutely right,
Merely a futile endeavor,
A testament to my folly!

# Appreciative Thankful Favored

Sincerely appreciative,
Are you?
Am I?
For the nourishment on our table,
Shelter above our heads,
Attire upon our forms.
Am I indebted for the provision from above?

Indeed, I do acknowledge and recognize
Your guidance,
Every instance, every day.

I persist in gratitude, sincerely!

Oh! How favored I feel,
For your divine kindness,
Your watchful care,
My joy, my contentment.
I am fortunate,
I am abundantly blessed,
I am at peace.

I shall forever remain
Appreciative, thankful, and favored.

# Legacy of a craftsman:
# Lesson from Papa

He crafted bamboo knitting needles,
Encircling wool around my fingers,
Guiding me to knit a muffler.

Positioning the chopping board,
Assisting me with a dao to cut a chicken,
Yet, neither of us could bring down a life
Chicken.

Teaching me to wield a hammer and nail,
Constructing picket fences,
But first, instructing me on the handling of a
saw.

The hands that now work on wood,
And Mason works too,
It was Papa,
Who taught me first!

You might say I'm crafty
Now you know where it is coming from!

# From Garden to Business

Just 8 years old,
Naughty, shy and Awkward
Consciously thought to myself,
"What would they say!"
But I dared not mess up with Papa!

Either join him in his mission,
Or don't even dare go near him
Lest he make you work
And earn some pennies

Forced to sit beside the shop,
Me and my sisters!
He made small bundles
of coriander leaves,
Grown from our garden.
God knows how we did the transaction,
Wonder how much we earned!!

How was I to know,
At 8 years,
He was teaching us
Entrepreneurship
Hard work,
Trade,
Business!

Today, I am here!
Work with my hands
Support myself,
Support others!

# Nothing goes to waste

From the storage room,
He found some leftover wood,
To craft a makeshift guitar
For us to strum and sing along,
That memory of the guitar lingers for years!

He fashioned a cajon box for my niece,
Out of the cutout pieces
From our production house.

Now she taps its rhythm while she sings.
Yes, even to this day!

Nothing was squandered four decades ago,
And nothing is wasted now!
Our storage brims!
He would say, "Someday...."
And behold, "someday"
Always found utility.

Never would I fret over a broken shoe.
Daddy would repair it without fail!
Ah, what reassurance!
Yesterday, I presented him with a basket full!!
All for repairs!

These are the ways,
The ways He shows love
Did he ever utter "I love you?"

But ah! Actions speak volumes!
And they grow louder by the day!

# Legacy of Diligence

Working tirelessly at 80?
Indeed he is!
In terms of hours,
He outpaces me!
Indolence isn't in his lexicon,
Daytime slumber eludes him,
Even on weekends!

I could never aspire
To half of what he embodies!

Yet, I yearn to glean wisdom at his feet,
What he imparts will be my legacy,
Truly, he lives a life of fulfillment.

Undoubtedly,
He's fashioning a legacy for me!

# JOY

Once in a while, Joy and happiness confuse me,
Not because I don't know,
But because of what was taught while I was
young.


That joy comes from within,
-From knowing Christ.
Happiness is something we attain
-from outside circumstances...

But for me, it's synonymous.

What makes you joyful?
-Flower blooming
-Creating pretty things
-Helping hands
-Making a child smile
-Seeing them fit.

What takes away the Joy?
I was once told,
With Jesus, there is Joy!
But where is Joy in down circumstances?

Can I be  happy or joyful
-When I am hurt?
-Back-stabbed?
-Cruelty to humans?
-And animals as well?
-When disaster strikes?
-What about when I'm financially broke?

What makes joy last?
Yes, having Jesus and living as one
- The Ultimate Joy!

These do matter—
-Balanced life
-Positive thought pattern
-Staying focussed
-Doing what makes me happy
-Good friends

What gives you the greatest joy?
Above everything else,
Definitely,
The joy of the Lord is my strength
And THAT is my greatest JOY!

# Silent Mentor

A decade of companionship,
Understanding
Deep
Profound.

He believed in my worth,
When I was blind to see myself.

He envisioned greatness within,
Guided me to heights unseen,
Though my wings were yet to unfurl.

Constructive critique,
A relentless push,
Strengthening me through the pain,
For excellence was his sole aim,
Perhaps, glimpsing the path ahead,
Aware his time was fleeting,
A silent mentor,
Shaping my journey.

# Bridging the gap :
# A DIVINE CALL

A decade,
A divine assignment,
To be his earthly guardian,
Advocate to authority
Clients
Kin
Even to healers' ears.

I may have prayed less,
But this I know,
I was called to bridge the gap.

Times of distress,
His plea,
A call I heeded,
Beyond my means,
In service,
Exceeding capacity.
I did what I thought best.

Wreath on his coffin
Flowers around him
Testimony in front of the people
It was a pleasure to do it all.
My decade of a guardian angel
Came to a closure then!

# Portrait of a Noble Soul

What can I say about him?
He was gentle,
He was a perfectionist,
He was talented,
He was considerate,
He was ambitious,
He was hardworking.
He was a happy Prince!

And one thing he was,
He was never willing
To give up on life!

He knew when to keep quiet,
And when to speak out!
Gossip was a no no!
No one could speak ill of his friends
He would defend his friends,
Even fight for them!

He loved his siblings and mum much more!
What he did not know—
He didn't know how to tell!
But he sure had a pure heart,
Only his smile said it all.

# Beyond Earthly Bounds

He had his shortfalls,
But he had his confidence!

But confidence was not all
To face this fierce world.

And what he needed,
the world couldn't give!

He was ambitious,
Far beyond understanding.

Maybe, he was meant for Heaven!
Maybe, heaven needed him more.

# Legacy of Light

Today, he's departed,
But his smile endures,
His guidance,
And his faith in me.

I'll ascend as he desired,
His memory etched in legacy,
A life remembered,
Though now past.

Farewell my friend, till we meet again.

# My Life - My Time

I've often heard these words,
Deeply ingrained in my heart,
My time with you is valuable,
Not merely valuable!

My time with you is utterly priceless,
Unbuyable by any,
Unfit for wastefulness,
And untouchable by misuse!

Has anyone shared with you
That time is synonymous with life?
Time once used cannot be regained,
Just as your life passes by.

When I grant you my time,
I bestow upon you a part of my life,
And that fleeting moment,
Is lost forever,
Never to return!

Truly,
My time is unequivocally precious,
Seize the present.
How will you expand your life?
How will you utilize your time?

# Journeys

The journeys we embarked on,
Oh, countless they became,
Under the scorching summer sun,
Amidst bustling traffic and endless queues,
Through the weary waiting and drowsy hours,
Yet you stood by me,
Helpless yet hopeful,
And through it all,
I recall vividly,
Mother, your smile never waned.

Yes, from one doctor's office to the next,
Endless rest and numerous tests,
Through seasons changing,
You and I, seeking wellness,
Enduring those rides together.

# Watching You Fade

Mama, were you aware of what I couldn't see?
Did you realize you were slipping away?
When you smiled at them,
What was going through your mind?
During those medical visits,
What thoughts occupied you?

Hope against all odds,
Through seasons passing,
I'm certain you wished for wellness,
Longed for life.

I recall that morning,
Your hesitation
To embark on those journeys once more.
No one else was home,
Just you and I,
The bitter tears I shed
While packing your bags
For yet another trip,
Hoping for recovery.

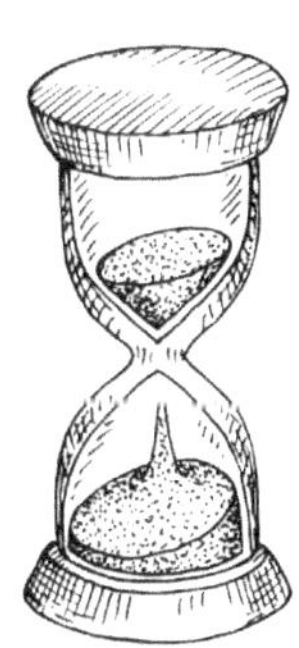

But alas,
You were slipping,
Growing frail,
Losing yourself,
Drifting from reality.

# Empty Arms, Aching Heart

Empty arms, aching heart
As you drifted from reality,
As you recognised only me,
As restlessness took hold,
Did you sense your fading?

What thoughts filled your mind
When prayers brought solace,
When hymns brought melody,
Did you perceive your fading?

When chewing became a challenge,
When your mouth stayed closed,
When your words became unintelligible,
Did you feel your fading?

When I promised a swift return,
When you waved goodbye that morning,
When I assured you of my imminent return,
Did you realize I'd never see you alive?

Oh mother!
My heart aches deeply,
Your hands were warm as I left,
When I promised to return,
You didn't wait for me.

Your hands had grown icy by the time I
returned,
You left before my arrival,
Why, mother? Why?
My heart continues to ache,
You've left an unfathomable void,
Why, mother, why?

# Unfolding Story

She is reserved yet playful,
Serene yet vibrant with energy,
Often filled with giggles.

She enjoys crafting with wood and bamboo,
Takes pleasure in coloring pictures,
Quick in picking up new skills!
Oh, how I envision collaborating with her on
craft projects one day!

She shows promise as a leader,
A devoted and affectionate daughter,
A wonderful companion
And always ready to lend a hand.

She is now seven,
And I look forward to watching
her mature,
Growing in years, knowledge,
and stature,
Gaining favor with both God
and people,
Discovering her life's purpose,
And embracing God's plans for her future.

# Always returning back to You

It's that familiar smile,
The tender, yearning smile,
Sometimes accompanied by open arms,
Like a delighted father welcoming
His daughter, taking her first steps,
As she hurries towards him.

Ah, that comforting embrace
Of the father!
Yet, the daughter—
Restless, always wandering—
Steps out once more,
While the father waits,
Patiently yearning,
For her return.

That's me,
And that's Him,
I won't keep wandering,
Not a wanderer,
I will always return to Him,
Back to His welcoming embrace.

# Loyal Companion

By my side, through thick and thin,
A loyal friend, with fur and grin.
With every wag, a tale is spun,
In your eyes, a love that's won.

With tangling of the car key,
you are there, following me,
Hoping that I would take you out.

With the shut of the door,
You come rushing,
To hold the keys.
Always there to pick up parcels,
Always there to obey orders.

Loyalty is your nickname, companionship is
your motto,
Your purpose in life is to set my heart aglow.
How do you even know I love you!

So here's to you, my faithful friend,
On this journey that seems to have no end.
With every moment, our bond grows strong,
In your friendship, I forever belong.

# Sisters of the Soul

In the tapestry of life, they weave,
Threads of faith,
Of love,
Of grace.

Through trials faced,
They never leave,
In their presence, a sacred space.

Bound not by blood, but by divine,
They walk together, hand in hand.
Through laughter shared, they intertwine,
In their unity, a promise grand.

In moments of joy and moments of sorrow,
They lift each other, heart and soul.
With prayers whispered for a better tomorrow,
In their bond, a strength untold.

They don't always meet,
Yet connected by a higher calling.
In their embrace, hearts aglow,
In their journey, a sacred falling.

So let their sisterhood shine bright,
A constellation in the night.
In their love, there is no blight,
In their unity, they find their light.

# A Friendship Lament

In bonds of friendship,
Toxic weeds may grow,
Their thorns unseen,
Their roots entwined below.

What once was pure,
Now tainted by deceit,
As poison whispers in the words we greet.

A friend turned foe,
Disguised in guise of care,
Their venom spreads,
Infecting all we share.

Their envy blooms,
A flower dark and cold,
Within the garden of our friendship bold.

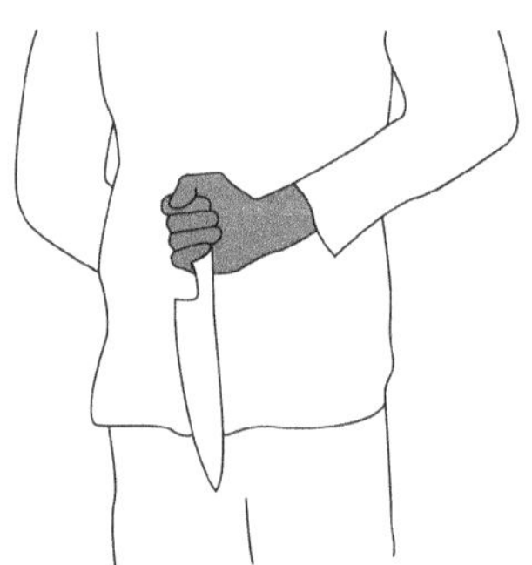

Yet hope remains, in hearts that dare to mend,
To prune away the poison, to amend.
For true companionship, though rare to find,
Brings healing rains to nourish weary minds.

So let us sift through soil of trust and strife,
To cultivate the friendships worth our life.
For in the end, though trials we may face,
True friendship blooms in love's enduring grace.

# Not Just Behind the Pulpit

From pulpit's high, where echoes ring,
To humble studios where workers laugh,
The calling comes in varied guise,
In every corner, it does rise.

Not only in the preacher's words,
But also where the toil is heard,
In offices and factory floors,
Where daily tasks the spirit soars.

For there, amid the daily grind,
A sacred purpose we may find,
To shine a light in the darkest hour,
And spread compassion's gentle power.

In a work-place where the vulnerable meet,
Where insecure becomes confident,
The blind sees their worth,
Hopelessness finds a meaning.

In rooms filled with stress and strife,
Or fields where labor shapes a life,
The ministry of work takes flight,
In deeds that turn the wrong to right.

So let us heed the silent call,
To serve with love, to stand tall,
For in each task, in every role,
We find the essence of the soul.

# Unbound Grace

In solitude's embrace, she stands,
An aura of strength, a soul untamed.
Through trials faced with steady hands,
In her essence, a fire unclaimed.

No chains to bind, no limits set,
She walks her path with fearless stride.
With every challenge, she's met,
In her heart, a spirit untried.

Through valleys deep and mountains high,
She forges onward, undeterred.
Beneath the vast and endless sky,
In her presence, courage conferred.

Her voice resounds, a melody pure,
A symphony of resilience and grace.
With every step, she does endure,

In her independence, a sacred space.

So let her light shine bright and free,
A beacon for all who dare to see.
In her strength, she finds her glee,
In her independence, she is truly free.

# Guiding Light

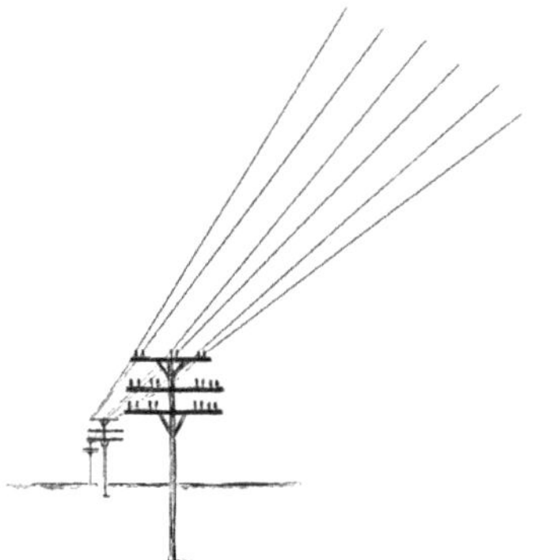

In life's vast sea, where shadows roam,
A beacon shines, a guiding light.
Through tempests fierce, we find our home,
In wisdom's glow, our future's bright.

A mentor's hand, a steady guide,
In every step, their wisdom clear.
Through highs and lows, they stand beside,
In every doubt, their voice we hear.

With courage forged from their embrace,
We brave the storms, we chart our course.
In their footsteps, we find our grace,
In their teachings, we find our force.

Their legacy, a flame aglow,
Ignites our hearts, inspires our quest.

In their example, we learn and grow,
In their presence, we find our best.

So let us cherish those who lead,
Whose influence shapes our destiny.
In their footsteps, we plant our seed,
In their love, we find our harmony.

# Eternal Echoes of Friendship

In childhood's golden days, we roamed,
Two kindred souls, our hearts entwined.
Through laughter, tears, and dreams we soared,
In innocence, our bond defined.

But now, my friend, your light grows dim,
As cancer's shadow steals your grace.
Though time may fade, our memories swim,
In every smile, your gentle face.

With each passing day, a battle fought,
Yet courage shines within your eyes.
Though pain may linger, hope is sought,
As wings of love embrace the skies.

In childhood's garden, we once played,
In fleeting moments, we still dance.

Though seasons change, our bond won't fade,
In every heartbeat, our friendship's trance.
We are far apart now, only He knows if we shall meet.
But one thing I am glad, you and I have found our peace,
You and Him have found your peace.
Happily, you go ahead, until He calls me back to you

So let this poem be a gentle song,
A tribute to the love we share.
Though earthly paths may not be long,
In spirit's realm, we'll meet in Heaven.

# HANDS

Have you seen the hands of men,
That abuse, steal, and destroy?
From slaps to theft, they find their way,
To harm, to hurt, day by day.

But what of God, in His divine plan?
His hands create, His miracles span.
With comfort and care, He gently holds,
And in His grasp, our faith unfolds.

His hands release blessings, not a curse,
Creating, healing, no soul to coerce.
With every touch, a life restored,
His love, His grace, forever adored.

So let my hands, in humble plea,
Be instruments of His love, you see.
To offer aid, to give, to mend,
In His image, my hands extend.

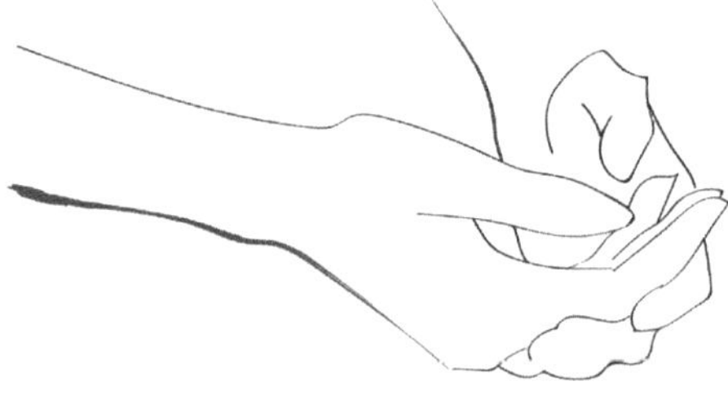

# Co-creator

In Genesis' pages, a tale unfurls,
Of two creators shaping worlds.
Beside the Divine, I stand tall,
Crafting visions, answering the call.

In the canvas of my business,
they forge anew,
Dreams and ideas, bold and true.
With God's guidance and human hands,
Enterprises rise in fertile lands.

From chaos to order, they bring forth light,
Navigating challenges, day and night.
In partnership with the divine,
I carve their grand design.

Like artisans of old, I construct and paint,
Until the beauty come alive,
For you and me to enjoy the sight,
And rejoice together with the divine.
In Genesis' echoes, their story is told,
Co-creators with God, in ventures bold.

So let me heed the call,
May you hear and respond too
To create, to innovate, to stand tall.
For in the heart of Genesis' lore,
Lies the blueprint for dreams to soar.

# A Milestone

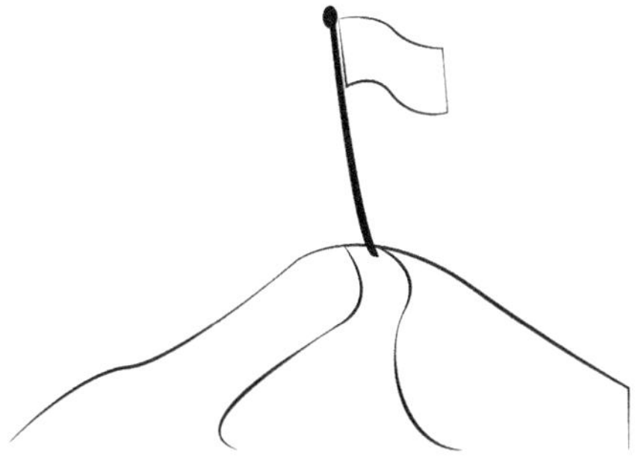

I am a traveler,
Have journeyed for many years.
The paths were not always smooth,
Nor were they overly difficult,
Just within the limits of my strength.

Traveled enough to understand,
To bend down and reassure it's alright,
To stand tall and show the way

Traveled enough to witness births,
To care for the sick,
To comfort the wounded
And to witness a few deaths too!

I have journeyed extensively,
Life has consistently been my teacher,
Learning so I can guide others,

Failing so I can advise caution,
Succeeding so I remain humble

Yes, this is my milestone year,
Looking back and thinking,
Ah, it wasn't so challenging after all!
Looking ahead and saying,
Well, I'm eagerly anticipating what's to come!